What Is Lent?

Preparing for Easter

What Is Lent?

Copyright © 2011 by Abingdon Press
All rights reserved.

No part of this work may be reproduced or transmitted in any form or by any means, electronic or mechanical, including photocopying and recording, or by any information storage or retrieval system, except as may be expressly permitted by the 1976 Copyright Act or by permission in writing from the publisher.
Requests for permission should be addressed in writing to: Abingdon Press, Permissions Office, 201 Eighth Avenue, South, P.O. Box 801, Nashville, TN 37202-0801; faxed to (615) 749-6128; or sent via e-mail to *permissions@abingdonpress.com*.

Scripture quotations in this publication, unless otherwise indicated, are from the New Revised Standard Version of the Bible, copyright 1989, Division of Christian Education of the National Council of the Churches of Christ in the United States of America. Used by permission. All rights reserved.

Written by Marcia Stoner

Janet Patterson Karns, Production Editor
Keitha Vincent, Designer

Art Credits—pp. 7, 14-15, 24: © Shutterstock; pp. 16, 28: (palm branch): Rick Drennan / Storybook Arts, © 2008 Cokesbury; pp. 17 (towel and basin), 20 (black-draped cross): Randy Wollenmann, © 2008 Cokesbury; pp. 17 (bread and cup), 18, 19, 21, 28 (cross), 29 (rooster, crown of thorns): Randy Wollenmann, © 2003 Cokesbury; p. 17 (grapes and wheat): Randy Wollenmann, © 2009 Cokesbury; p. 20 (nails): Nervene Covington, © 2002 Cokesbury; p. 28 (tomb): Dennis Jones, © 2001 Cokesbury; pp. 28 (butterfly), 29 (phoenix, egg, peacock, lily): Randy Wollenmann, © 2001 Cokesbury

ISBN 978-1-426-70848-0

PACP00502392-05

14 15 16 17 18 19 20 - 10 9 8 7 6 5

Manufactured in the United States of America

CONTENTS

What Is Lent? 4

He Was Tempted 5

Counting the Days 6

Last Tuesday Before Lent............................7

First Day of Lent 8

A Time to Repent...........9

Giving Up / Adding To 10–11

Holy Week 12

Holy Week Quiz 13

Holy Week Timeline 14–15

Symbols of Holy Week ...16

Last Supper Symbols ...17

Symbols of Denial and Betrayal 18

Symbols of Humiliation 19

Symbols of the Crucifixion and Death of Jesus ...20–21

The Last Day 22–23

Holy Week Services 24–27

The New Beginning...28–29

Answers 30–32

What Is Lent?

Lent is the period before Easter when we prepare our hearts for the resurrection of our Savior, Jesus.

Originally Lent was the time when converts to Christianity were instructed in the faith. This instruction prepared them for baptism. Often this baptism took place on Easter.

Lent reminds us of Jesus' time of fasting and temptation in the wilderness after his baptism. This is why Lent is considered a time of fasting and preparation.

Convert: a person who changes from one way of believing to another. A convert to Christianity is a person who has come to believe in Jesus as Lord.

He Was Tempted

In Matthew 4:1-11 we read that after his baptism Jesus spent forty days and nights in the wilderness fasting. At the end of this time Jesus was faced with three temptations that were to encourage him to take up his place as the Son of God with all the power and glory that goes with that. Jesus knew this was not God's plan.

Jesus was challenged to:

1. change stones into loaves of bread
2. throw himself off the Temple allowing angels to save him
3. fall down and worship the devil so that he could rule the world

Jesus resisted these three temptations, relying on God's word to make him known at the proper time.

Name three things that tempt you away from following God.

1. _____

2. _____

3. _____

Counting the Days

Lent begins with Ash Wednesday. (That's right! It begins in the middle of the week.) And it lasts forty days, ending on the Saturday before Easter.

If you've done your counting, you know that adds up to more than forty days. Something's not right. Solve the puzzle below to discover how forty days are reached and the reason why. (Some numbers aren't used.)

A = 1	G = 4	N = 7	U = 10
B = 2	I = 5	O = 8	V = 11
E = 3	J = 6	S = 9	Y = 12

__ __ N D __ __ __ __ R __ __ __ T C __ __ __ __ T __ D , __ __
9 10   1 12 9   1   3 7 8   8 10 7   3   1 9

T H __ __ __ R __ C __ __ __ __ D __ R __ D __ M __ LL
   3 12 1   3   8 7 9 5   3   3   9   1

C __ L __ __ R __ T __ __ __ __ __ F __ __ __ T __ R .
  3   3 2 1   5 8 7 9 8   3 1 9   3

(Answers are on p. 30)

Last Tuesday Before Lent

The Tuesday before Lent begins was originally called "Shrove Tuesday." The word *shrove* is the past tense of *shrive,* which means "to hear confessions."

Since Lent was a time of penance (confessing) and fasting, people didn't have parties or eat rich foods such as butter, milk, and eggs during Lent. Since people couldn't afford to waste food, what did they do?

On the Tuesday before Lent began they would use up all these foods. It's even been said that people ate more than the usual number of meals on this day. Since so many foods with fats were consumed, the day became known to many as "Fat Tuesday."

Never heard of Fat Tuesday? You really have if you've heard of Mardi Gras. *Mardi Gras* is French for Fat Tuesday. Even though some people may not observe the religious meaning of the day, the parties and celebration come to an abrupt end with the beginning of Lent.

Unscramble the word below to figure out what people traditionally serve for Shrove Tuesday.

N K A S P C E A

_ _ _ _ _ _ _ _

(Answers are on p. 30.)

First Day of Lent

Fat Tuesday is past; the parties are over. The serious season of Lent begins. The first day of Lent is called Ash Wednesday. The Ash Wednesday worship service is the first act of Lent.

Circle all the numbers below that correctly describe Ash Wednesday. If you choose well, the numbers will add up to 10!

1. Ash Wednesday is named for the ashes placed on the worshipper's forehead.

2. Ash Wednesday services are followed by the eating of a special unleavened bread.

3. Anything may be burned to make the ashes for the service.

4. Placing ashes in the form of a cross on the forehead is an act of public repentance.

5. The service helps focus the season of Lent on repentance.

6. The practice of holding an Ash Wednesday service is a modern tradition.

(Answers are on p. 30.)

A Time to Repent

During Lent we prepare our hearts and minds to live as disciples of Christ. Part of this preparation is repentance.

To repent is to be sincerely sorry for wrongdoing and to want to be in a better relationship with God. There is something else it means. Follow the lines and write the letters at the end of each in the blanks below to discover what else we must do to truly repent. (The word will be written backward.)

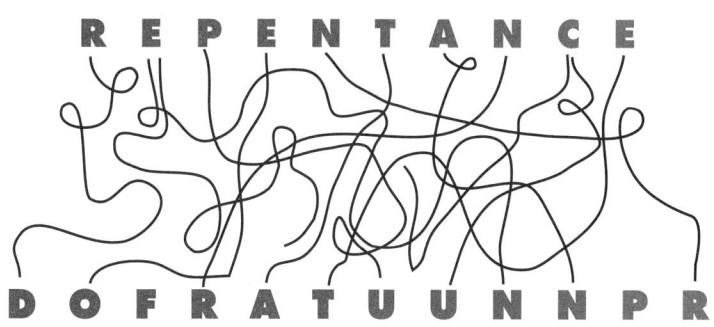

___ ___ ___ ___ ___ ___ ___ ___ ___

and try to live more faithfully.

(Answers are on p. 30.)

Giving Up

To remind themselves that Jesus went without food in the wilderness for forty days and nights, many people give up something during the season of Lent. Often it is a favorite food.

In the word search below, find things people give up or add to their lives during Lent. (The list is on page 11. Look for the words in **bold**.)

```
B I B L E R E A D I N G L
D P A F E C O L O R F G Y
A P R A Y E R M O V I E S
I I K V M M I J F D L M S
L J O U R N A L I N G A C
Y K I N D N E S S N Y G A
S E R V I C E J K N E P A
```

(Answers are on p. 30.)

Adding To

Churches take time during Lent to study the life and teachings of Jesus. To be faithful to Jesus' teachings, many people add something extra to enrich their spiritual lives during the season of Lent. Others will do both—give up something and add something.

Put a *G* before the things people would give up and an *A* for the things people would add to their spiritual lives during Lent.

___ extra **Bible reading**

___ favorite **food**

___ **journaling**

___ wearing favorite **color**

___ perform a **daily** act of **kindness**

___ **service** project

___ **movies**

___ favorite **game**

___ extra **prayer** time

(Answers are on p. 30.)

HOLY WEEK

We are all familiar with Palm Sunday, the day that celebrates Jesus' triumphal entry into Jerusalem. This joyful celebration gives way to much more serious remembrances of the last week of Jesus' life.

Three important days of Holy Week:

HOLY (MAUNDY) THURSDAY
This is the day the disciples and Jesus arrive at the upper room for the washing of feet and the celebration of the Last Supper.

Maundy probably comes from Latin and means "mandate" (commandment).

GOOD FRIDAY (*good* in old English also means "holy")
This commemorates the crucifixion and death of Jesus on the cross.

HOLY SATURDAY
Often seen as the last sabbath for the disciples as Jews. The resurrection of Jesus on Sunday is seen as the time Jesus' closest disciples became "Christians."

HOLY WEEK

Put an **X** in front of the events that are commemorated during Holy Week.

_____ The birth of Jesus

_____ Jesus' triumphal entry into Jerusalem

_____ Jesus washes the disciples feet.

_____ Jesus and the disciples share Jesus' last supper.

_____ Jesus gives the Sermon on the Mount.

_____ Jesus is betrayed by Judas.

_____ Jesus prays in the garden of Gethsemane.

_____ Jesus is arrested.

_____ Jesus is crucified.

_____ The Holy Spirit descends at Pentecost.

(Answers are on p. 31.)

HOLY WEEK timeline

SUNDAY	MONDAY	TUESDAY	WEDNESDAY
Jesus enters Jerusalem on a donkey.	Jesus cleanses the Temple.	Jesus teaches in the Temple. Mary of Bethany anoints Jesus' feet.	Judas agrees to betray Jesus (this may have happened on Wednesday).

THURSDAY	FRIDAY	SATURDAY
Jesus washes disciples' feet.	Jesus is betrayed and arrested.	Jesus is in the tomb.
Jesus and his disciples eat the Last Supper in the upper room.	Jesus is tried.	
	Jesus is crucified.	
Jesus prays in the garden of Gethsemane.	Jesus is buried.	

Symbols of Holy Week

There are a lot of symbols that remind us of all the events of Holy Week.

The first symbols are the **palm branch** and **cloak**. People laid palm branches and cloaks on the road before Jesus to honor him.

Unscramble the words below to learn what title the people gave Jesus as he rode into Jerusalem.

SNO   FO   VDDIA

___   ___   _____

(Answers are on p. 31.)

Last Supper Symbols

In the upper room, Jesus demonstrated how to serve by washing the feet of his disciples. The basin and towel have become the symbols of servanthood.

"While they were eating, Jesus took a loaf of bread, and after blessing it he broke it, gave it to the disciples, and said, 'Take, eat; this is my body.'"
(Matthew 26:26)

"Then he took a cup, and after giving thanks he gave it to them, saying, 'Drink from it, all of you; for this is my blood of the covenant, which is poured out for many for the forgiveness of sins.'"
(Matthew 26:27-28)

Symbols of Denial and Betrayal

Two of Jesus' disciples let him down on the night he was arrested. Match the symbol with the description of the denial/betrayal and the disciple.

One disciple betrayed Jesus to the authorities in exchange for thirty pieces of silver.

Because he was afraid, one disciple denied knowing Jesus three times on the night of Jesus' arrest.

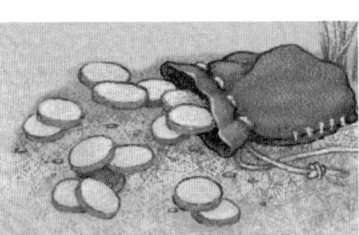

PETER

JUDAS

RESULTS:
The one who betrayed Jesus to the authorities regretted it and committed suicide.

The one who denied Jesus three times repented. He never denied knowing Jesus again, even though his faithfulness later resulted in his own crucifixion.

(Answers are on p. 31.)

Symbols of Humiliation

SCOURGE
Pilate ordered that Jesus be flogged before he was turned over for crucifixion.

Read Matthew 27:15-26 to learn about Pilate's role in Jesus' trial.

CROWN OF THORNS
The soldiers took Jesus and, to mock him, made a crown of thorns.

Read Matthew 27:27-31 to learn more about Jesus' humiliation.

KING OF THE JEWS
To mock Jesus further, they made an inscription for his cross.

Read Luke 23:32-38 to learn about Jesus' suffering.

Symbols of the Crucifixion

The Crucifixion is the darkest day in Christian history.

NAILS are a symbol of the Crucifixion because a large nail would have been driven through Jesus' feet. It is thought that nails were also driven through his hands. (In John 20:24-29, Thomas asks to see Jesus' hands.)

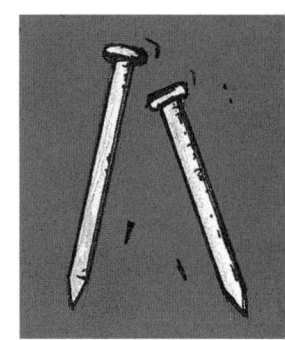

BLACK-DRAPED CROSS: Jesus was crucified on a cross. A cross draped with black is a symbol of the crucifixion and death of Jesus.

Crucifixion was a very horrible way to die.

and Death of Jesus

SEALED TOMB: After Jesus died on the cross he was buried and sealed in a tomb.

The tomb did not belong to Jesus or his family. It was offered as Jesus' burial place. To which of these people did the tomb belong?

Mary Magdalene, Simon of Cyrene, Joseph of Arimathea

(Answer is on p. 32.)

The Last Day

Many things happened on the day Jesus was arrested. And these events happened very quickly.

Jesus prayed in the garden of Gethsemane and immediately afterward was betrayed by Judas and arrested.

Jesus was then taken before the high priest and the council. While Jesus was before the council, Peter denied Jesus three times. The cock (rooster) crowed three times.

What happened next? We've put the timeline for Jesus' last day on page 23.

Mark 15:25 tells us that Jesus was crucified at nine o'clock in the morning. Matthew and John tell us when darkness descended and what happened at three o'clock. Other times are figured from these and other clues in the Bible.

6:00 A.M.	Jesus is taken before Pilate and sent to Herod. (Mark 15:1-5, Luke 23:6-10)
7:00 A.M.	Jesus is returned to Pilate. Pilate orders Jesus flogged and then sentences him to crucifixion. (Luke 23:11-25)
8:00 A.M.	Jesus is led to Golgotha, and Simon of Cyrene is called upon to help carry the cross. (Luke 23:26)
9:00 A.M.	Jesus is nailed to the cross. (Mark 15:25, Luke 23:33)
10:00 A.M.	Jesus forgives those crucifying him. Soldiers divide Jesus' clothes. (Luke 23:34)
11:00 A.M.	Jesus tells a criminal crucified beside him, "Today you will be with me in Paradise." (Luke 23:43)
12:00 P.M.	Darkness descends. Jesus gives his mother into John's care. (Mark 15:33, John 19:26-27)
3:00–4:00 P.M.	• Jesus says, "My God, my God, why have you forsaken me?" (Matthew 27:46) • Jesus says, "I am thirsty." (John 19:28) • Jesus says, "It is finished" and "Father, into your hands I commend my spirit." (John 19:30, Luke 23:46)

Sometime between 3:00 and 5:00 P.M., Jesus dies. There is an earthquake, and the curtain of the Temple is torn in two. (John 19:30, Luke 23:46, Matthew 27:51)

5:00 P.M.   Jesus' side is pierced with a spear.
Jesus is buried before the sun goes down.

Holy Week Services

The most important worship services of the Christian Year are held during Holy Week and on Easter morning.

Work the puzzle to discover the names of some of these services and/or the days on which they are held.

ACROSS

3. When you write or speak you use these.
4. Opposite of *first*
7. Trains pull into these.
9. This one's hard. It begins with a *T* and ends with an *E* and it's a word you may not know.
10. The day before Sunday.
11. "Walk this _____."
    "Come this _____."
    "Get out of the _____."
    "I know the _____. I can get there."

DOWN

1. Jesus was crucified on this.
2. Type of tree branch
5. The number that comes between six and eight
6. Opposite of "bad"
8. The day after Wednesday

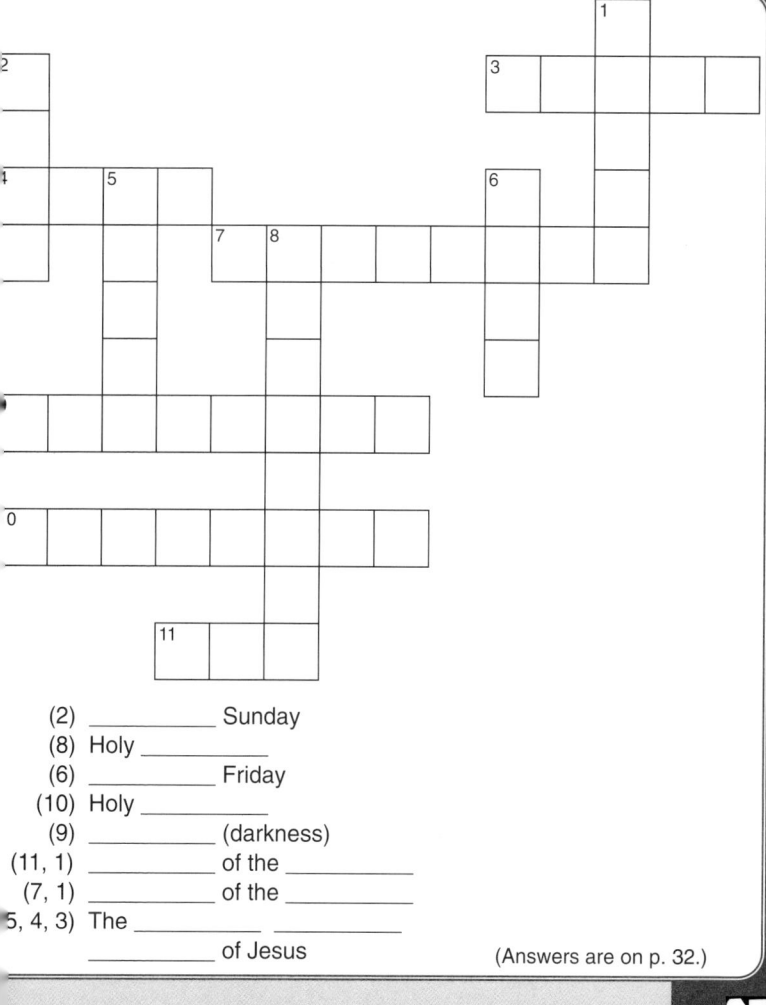

(2) _____ Sunday
(8) Holy _____
(6) _____ Friday
(10) Holy _____
(9) _____ (darkness)
(11, 1) _____ of the _____
(7, 1) _____ of the _____
(5, 4, 3) The _____ of _____ _____ of Jesus

(Answers are on p. 32.)

25

The PALM SUNDAY worship service is the happiest of the season of Lent. Processions of people waving palm branches are often held and are often led by children. This service is a time of joy and celebration. It is held in honor of Jesus' triumphal entry into Jerusalem.

The HOLY THURSDAY worship service celebrates the Last Supper (Passover meal) of Jesus and his disciples. Some churches ask a rabbi to come and serve a Seder (Passover) meal.

Holy Thursday services can also include a foot-washing and Communion. (John 13:1-17; Matthew 26:26-35)

Another Holy Thursday or Good Friday service is the SERVICE OF TENEBRAE (Service of the Shadows). Fourteen candles and a central Christ candle (always white) are lighted. There are fourteen readings telling the story of Jesus' arrest, trial, and crucifixion. After each reading a candle is extinguished. Then there is a reading about Jesus' death, and the Christ candle is extinguished. A loud noise is made, and then in total darkness a reading of the story of Jesus' burial is read. Everyone leaves in silence.

The GOOD FRIDAY worship service may be done in several ways (Tenebrae, Seven Last Words, or other readings). At the end of the Good Friday service everything is removed from the altar except the cross. The cross is often veiled or draped with a black cloth.

On HOLY SATURDAY, churches may hold one of two types of service: The Seven Last Words or The Way of the Cross (also known as Stations of the Cross).

The SEVEN LAST WORDS is a worship service based upon readings of the seven things Jesus said from the cross.

THE WAY OF THE CROSS is a way of experiencing the full story of the Crucifixion. In the church or outdoors, stops (or stations) are set up in different locations. At each of these there is a reminder of part of Jesus' "way to the cross." There are fourteen of these stations, from Jesus in the garden of Gethsemane to Jesus' burial. There may be Bible readings or other ways of worshiping at each station. Sometimes people go through the stations in a group, and sometimes people go through individually and read the Bible and pray at each stop.

The New Beginning

Lent ends on the Saturday before Easter. The reflection and penance of Lent are over. Easter Sunday arrives, and the altar is usually decked out with an empty cross (or a flowered cross) and white lilies. We celebrate the resurrection of Jesus. This is the single most important day of the year for Christians.

Some of the symbols on these two pages are Easter symbols and some are not. Circle the letter beside each Easter symbol. Then unscramble the letters to learn what Easter symbols stand for.

(Answers are on p. 32)

_ _ _ _   _ _ _ _ (Answers are on p. 32.)

ANSWERS

"Counting the Days" (p. 6): Sundays are not counted, as they are considered small celebrations of Easter.

"Last Tuesday Before Lent" (p. 7): PANCAKES

"First Day of Lent" (p. 8): 1, 4, and 5

"A Time to Repent" (p. 9): TURN AROUND (try to do things differently)

"Giving Up/Adding To" (pp. 10-11):

G (giving up): favorite food, wearing favorite color, movies, favorite game

A (adding to): extra Bible reading, journaling, perform a daily act of kindness, service project, extra prayer time

"Holy Week Quiz" (p. 13):
Holy Week Events: :
Jesus' triumphal entry into Jerusalem
Jesus washes the disciples' feet.
Jesus and the disciples share Jesus' last supper.
Jesus is betrayed by Judas.
Jesus prays in the garden of Gethsemane.
Jesus is arrested.
Jesus is crucified.

"Symbols of Holy Week" (p. 16): SON OF DAVID

"Symbols of Denial and Betrayal" (p.18):

One disciple betrayed Jesus to the authorities in exchange for thirty pieces of silver.

JUDAS

Because he was afraid, one disciple denied knowing Jesus three times on the night of Jesus' arrest. PETER

"Symbols of the Crucifixion and Death of Jesus" (pp. 20-21):
Joseph of Arimathea

"Holy Week Services" (pp. 24-25):

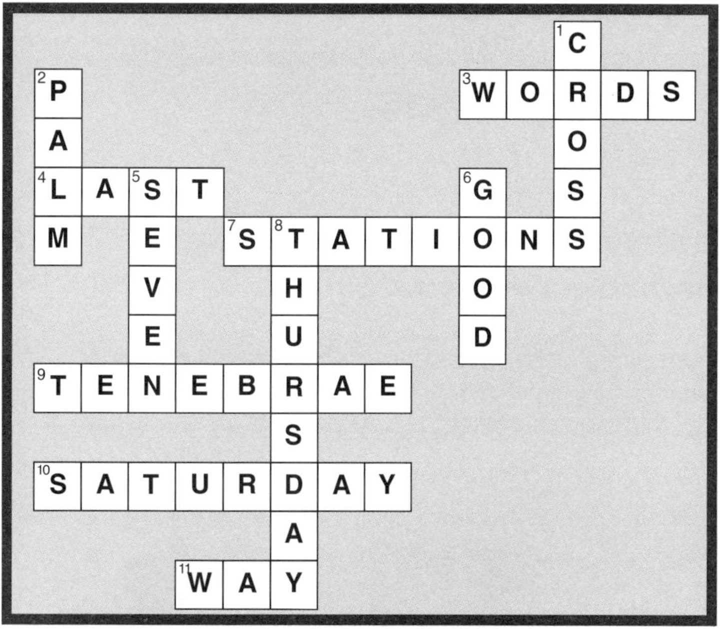

								¹C		
	²P				³W	O	R	D	S	
	A							O		
⁴L	A	⁵S	T			⁶G		S		
M		E		⁷S	⁸T	A	T	I	O	N	S
		V			H			O		
		E			U			D		
⁹T	E	N	E	B	R	A	E			
					S					
¹⁰S	A	T	U	R	D	A	Y			
					A					
		¹¹W	A	Y						

Palm Sunday, Holy Thursday, Good Friday, Holy Saturday, Tenebrae, Way of the Cross, Stations of the Cross, Seven Last Words of Jesus

"The New Beginning" (pp. 28-29): NEW LIFE—The palm branch, rooster, and crown of thorns are Lenten symbols. All others are symbols of new life, which is what we are offered at Easter. So they are Easter symbols.